Our
Naked
Souls

OUR NAKED SOULS

Andrews McMeel Publishing
a division of Andrews McMeel Universal
1130 Walnut Street, Kansas City, Missouri 64106

www.andrewsmcmeel.com

20 21 22 23 24 BVG 10 9 8 7 6 5 4 3 2 1

ISBN: 978-1-5248-6057-8

Library of Congress Control Number: 2020936658

Original design and cover by Justin Wetch
Cover illustrations © Shutterstock

Illustrator: Travis Kalani
Editor: Kevin Kotur
Production Editor: David Shaw
Production Manager: Cliff Koehler

ATTENTION: SCHOOLS AND BUSINESSES
Andrews McMeel books are available at quantity discounts with
bulk purchase for educational, business, or sales promotional use.
For information, please e-mail the Andrews McMeel Publishing
Special Sales Department: specialsales@amuniversal.com.

Our Naked Souls

Justin Wetch

Andrews McMeel
PUBLISHING®

Dedicated to the woman who showed me just how beautiful love can be.

Contents

Chapter One

Naked Souls

Defying Gravity

We could reach the skies
Together
If we only took the chance.

We could fly among the clouds
And touch the first rays
Of the rising sun.

We could fly forever up there
And never come back down
Defying gravity forever
An eternal dance transcending time.

Clovers

Love is found
By walking through
A vast field
Of clovers
Until you find
The one
With four leaves.

You make me feel
As lucky as can be.

Strength

The way you look at me
Gives me the strength
To fight through life
Far beyond what I ever thought possible.
You make me brave
You give me the strength
To keep going.

Forgotten How to Fly

To seek to control
The ones you love
Is a tragedy born
From the ashes of beauty;
Your love, once beautiful, once free
Is like a caged bird
Who has forgotten
How to fly

Do not destroy what you love
By trying to own it.

Day One

Where others told me
I was being unrealistic
Or laughed when I shared
My dreams,

You were the first
To take me seriously,
The only one
Who believed in my dreams.

You showed me love
Before anyone else
Thought anything of me.
I owe you everything.

Back to You

You have always been the one
I come back to

We stray from each other
Every now and again

But each time
We end up back here

I will always come
Back to you

You have always been the one
I wait for

Ping Pong

We were in and out of love
With each other
At different times
Never ready
To make something of us.

You Alone

With you
I hold back nothing.

I whisper to you
In my innermost voice
The voice of my truest self
Surrounded by the mighty walls
I have spent so long building
To keep everyone else out.

You are the only one
Who truly knows me.
You are the only one
I can truly be myself with.

Love Is Like Magic

Love is like magic:
It is limitless
And anything is possible
If you believe in it.

It's also like magic
In that the moment
You start to question it
To analyze it
To see how it works
It falls apart . . .

Love demands unshakable faith;
The more you believe in it
Without hesitation or vacillation
The more
Love
Transcends
Possibility.

The Tree of Life

Love is like a tree
Which, when planted on good soil
With rain and sunshine
Can live for hundreds of years.

But uproot the tree
And watch it shrivel away—
This is the natural tendency
Of the universe
And love is not immune;
Love, over time, decays to hate
If proper care is not taken
To make sure it thrives.

The deepest rewards of love
Cannot be reached
If sheer passion
Is not met
With hard work
And complete dedication.

The Eternity Between the Moments

Do you know that time
Stretches for an eternity
Between our moments
Of perception?

You can feel it
When you're in love
Or suffering heartbreak,
When you're amazed
By beauty
Or saddened
By suffering.

I could stay
In this moment
With you
Forever.

Fade Away

I fade away without your love
My colors dim and darken
I fall for you more every day
Without a hint of caution

Act II

Fairy tales teach you
That love is the end
Of a story,

That somehow
Lovers cross the horizon
Into the sunset
And everything is perfect forever.

No, love is the middle
Of a story.
It isn't a stasis
Of permanent starstruck eyes
And adoring hearts.

Love is the will
Of two people
To fight for the good
Between them
Even when it isn't easy.

Love is valuable
Not because it is won
But because
It is fought for.

A Love Like Yours

I have never felt a love like yours,
A love that could replace the sun,
A love that brightens my life
And makes me feel whole.

The silhouette of you
Against the cresting sun—
Somehow I knew, in that moment
That this is what love
Was always meant to look like.

Eloquent

Eloquent writers
Say more with less,

And you're the most
Eloquent of all.

You showed me an infinite love
Without a single word.

With only your eyes
You created a paradise.

Lying in Bed

The best thing in life
Is lying in bed with her
After a long day
Finding peace
In each other.

In that moment
Everything is still
Everything is okay.
The world stands still
As we lie together
Breathing warm hues of adoration
Eyes wide and full of wonder
For every time
Feels like the first.

I wouldn't trade
Even one
Of these many moments
For anything in the world.
There is nothing better
Than being so close
To the woman I love.

Justin Wetch

All the Small Pieces

I want to find
All the small pieces
Of my heart
That I have given away
In these many years.

I want to take them back
At any cost
So that I have more of myself
To give you.

Transcendence

When I can't see the good
In life
You shine
And show me
That true beauty still exists
And not all is darkness

You show me
That life can be more
Than mundane routines

You show me
How to embrace the sunlight
And feel the wind on my face

You show me
Transcendence.

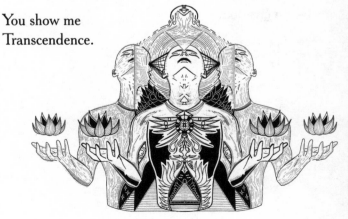

Justin Wetch

We Found Each Other

We found each other in the night
Not looking for love
Just needing to get away

We found each other by accident
And our love grew as if by magic
Where no one believed it could

Promise Me

I want to give you everything;
I want to throw myself into this
With everything I have,
But understand I've been hurt before
And it's not so easy for me.

So just promise me you mean it
When you tell me you love me.
Promise me you'll tell the truth
And not let me fall hard
If you're not ready to fall with me.

Completely

My greatest sorrow
Is that I will never be able to love her
As perfectly
As she deserves to be loved.

She loves my flaws
More beautifully
Than anyone else
Has loved
The best parts of me.

But if I can just reflect
Just a little bit
Of her,
Our love could light up
The universe.

Lucky One

The magical thing about us
Is that I think I'm the lucky one
To have you
And you think you're the lucky one
To have me.

We would both do anything
To keep each other.

Reincarnation

I like to think
That if reincarnation is real
We would still recognize each other
In our new forms.

I would know your soul anywhere
And would travel any distance
To reunite with you.

Who knows how many times
We already have?

Night

Flowers bloom in the night,
Glowing with an air of mystery

Somehow, gentle luminescence glows
Under the insanity of moonlight.
So too gleams the vulnerable seed
That grows between our clasped hands.

Drink deeply from this moment;
Let its infinity grace your soul
And promise me
You will hold a piece of it
Even when the night
Is over.

3:00 a.m.

I will never forget those nights
We spent
Just the two of us
Talking until three in the morning
Despite work
The next day

It was worth it
To live those moments
With you

Shades of Roses

With you
Life is shades of roses;
It glitters with gold
And shimmers with diamonds.

With you
The world seems at peace:

A glorious serenity
Sculpted from calamity.

Memory

Though I'll travel far
I will never forget you.
Though I'll live many years
Your memory will stay with me.
And though we might love others
Nothing could compare
To loving you.

My Love

When I am old, my love
And you are missing from our bed
And I make breakfast for one
Breathing in sorrow with the new day

When I am old, my love
And nothing tastes as sweet
Without you there with me
To love the world by my side

Will the bird songs
Still ring with glorious melody?
Will the smell of coffee
Still stir my soul to adventure?

When I am old, my love
Living on without you
I am not sure I will keep living
Though my heart still pumps blood.

For without you, my love
Life cannot truly go on
Just as the days would cease
Were the sun plucked from the sky.

Elevate

You do not require the extraordinary
To make things special.

You take the simplest things
And somehow elevate them.

You take the ordinary in life
And turn it into magic.

My Heart in Your Hands

My heart beats in your hands—
Please be careful.

I'm defenseless against you
Like no one else—
Please don't stab me
In the back.

I trust you
Like no one else—
Please don't take advantage.

I'm loyal to you
Like no one else—
Please don't make me
Look a fool.

I love you
Like no one else.
Please
Don't break me.

A Song for Just the Two of Us

Come with me
Up that winding road
Up to the mountains.

Let's lose ourselves
And forget our cares
If only for a day.

I'll bring my guitar
And you'll sing along
A song for just the two of us.

This Simple Love

Loving you
Was not something I expected
But a feeling that rose up
From deep within my soul
And overtook me
Like an ocean wave.

Swept up in this,
Let the ocean take us
Where it may.
All we need is each other,
All we need
Is this simple love.

Not Until

I will never run out
Of things to say about you;

My love for you
Springs in boundless eternity.

It will never falter
Nor weaken,

Not until the sun
Has run out of rays,

Not until the ocean
Has dried to a desert,

Not until the light
Has gone from my eyes.

We Never Fight

A perfect relationship
Is not one
Without conflict.

It is
Knowing how to deal
With conflict
In a mature and healthy way.

$C_{43}H_{66}N_{12}O_{12}S_2$

Just because a sunrise
Can be described
As the physics
Of our solar system
Causing the rotation of the earth
To make visible
The object around which it revolves
Doesn't change the fact
That a sunrise is beautiful.

In the same way
Just because something as beautiful
As love
Can be described as the influence of chemicals
In the brain
—a consequence of evolution—
Does not mean that's all there is to it.

Those who would deride love
As a mere chemical reaction
May be able to describe love
But will never understand it
Because the magic of being human
Is to synthesize transcendence
From the ordinary.

Jamais Vu

She turned monotony into novelty
Déjà vu into *jamais vu*
She made everything new
And nothing felt like it used to.

The simplest things took on new life
Grocery shopping felt like an adventure
Getting coffee was drinking the cosmos at night
And routines became vibrant pleasures.

She kissed me in the rain
As the city lights shone
I felt a warmth through my veins
As she painted night into glorious dawn.

With fresh eyes I looked at living
She effortlessly changed my point of view
Dear god, let me forever keep loving
La femme qui rend tout jamais vu.

Stars Align

What did the night's sky look like
At the moment of my first breath?
What did it look like
At the moment of yours?

I like to think
They were aligned perfectly
And perhaps if you combined them
Some cosmic echo of fate would be spelled out
In the depths of that abyss
And perhaps the future mapped already
In that ephemeral ink.

The night we met, our first words,
The moment I fell in love
With the details of your eyes,
Our first kiss,
The ever-closer intertwining
Of our souls,
And moments we haven't yet seen.

I don't know if the stars aligned
To bring us together.
All I know, my dear
Is that you make me feel
So damn lucky.

Lingua Franca

We must build a bridge
Between our love languages
So that I can speak enough of yours
And you enough of mine.

Understand that no two people
Perceive love exactly the same;
There are as many dialects of love
As there are perceptions of reality.

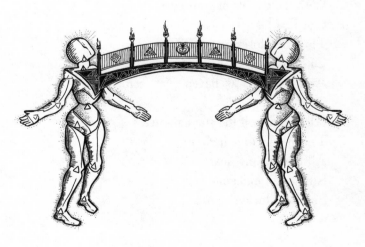

Look to the Stars

Look to the stars.
Incomprehensible vastness.

This great impossibility
Exists within you too,
In the space between your atoms.

You should look at yourself
With the same wonder
With which you look at the stars;
You, my love, are a miracle.

Accident

I refuse to believe that something as perfect
As the meeting of our souls
Could have happened
By accident.

Drive with Me

Drive with me.
Let's sing
At the top of our lungs
To songs we don't really know
Because every mistake
I make with you
Is beautiful.

Rest your head on my shoulder
And sleep through the sights
Like you sleep through movies
Because you're more beautiful
Falling asleep
Than the earth is
Dozing off at sunset.

Every single moment with you
Feels perfect
And the best of moments without you
Are lacking.

Drive with me
On to our next adventure
Because anything with you
Is perfect.

Brightest Star

Drive outside the city
In the midst of night.
Find a place
Where the stars
Shine with clarity.

Pick one out
And stare at it;
Watch as the stars around it
Grow dimmer
And all else
Becomes darkness.

This is what love
Is supposed to feel like;

Find the star
That looks brightest
To your soul
And never lose sight of it.

Aflame

Do not settle for someone
Whose soul is not aflame
With the music that moves you,
Eager to dance
In the same fire
That makes you feel
Alive.

Magic for the True Believer

The high tide
Wants to throw us
Against the rocks
And break us apart.

Love is a magic spell:
As long as we keep
Our eyes on each other
We'll never drown.

As long as we both believe
We can defy the odds
Somehow it becomes so;
Love is magic for the true believers.

Ourselves

Find someone who makes you
More and more yourself
Building you up
And erasing the scars
Where others had hurt you before.

I can be myself around you
And you yourself around me;
I think there's something beautiful
In that.

Fluorescent Infinity

Dip your fingers into the everlasting
Fluorescence.
Do not dare tell me
Magic does not exist
When I can feel it so strongly
Between us now.

But the moment the sunrise hits,
The harsh sobriety of the daylight hours
Lays waste to the infinite potential
Of the midnight hour.

We hold it all at bay,
God and goddess
Of our own infinity
Where everything we touch
Glows against the vast darkness.

We have infinite potential
In this moment—anything is possible
In this world we have created
Together.

In our world the sun
Never has
To rise.

My Heart Dreams of You

My heart never stopped dreaming of you
Even when all seemed lost.
Part of me never stopped belonging to you;
I don't think I could take it back if I tried.

My heart dreams of you
When I stare off into space
And lose track of time.

In the still, quiet moments
When the night is silent
And the air devoid of the slightest whisper,

In these quiet moments
Suddenly I find my heart
Drifting off to places
I had thought long abandoned.

What greater pain would be incurred:
To never wake up, having you only in fantasy,
Or to know for certain that this dream is a lie
Never to become reality?

Strands of Your Hair

I daydream about making you laugh,
Making your problems seem less daunting,
Cherishing the moments
As they float by in slow motion
And rush by in a blurry cascade
All at once.

I daydream about the small moments,
The way it would feel
When you leaned your head
Onto my shoulder
And I put my arm
Around your waist.

I think about how
I would find
Strands of your hair
In a shirt you had borrowed
And think fondly
About you
Every time.

Nothing but You and Me

Take my hand,
Lead me gently into oblivion;
You convince me that anything is possible,
That life can be more than ordinary.

You give me hope.
You fuel the fire deep down in my soul.

I look into your eyes
And for once it seems
That one day it will all make sense
And all of the struggle and pain
Will one day fade away,
Leaving nothing in the entire universe
But you and me.

There is beauty over the horizon,
A promise of harmony and joy;
To kiss you
Is to feel heaven
Touching earth.

When we are together
It feels as if there is nothing
But you and me
In the entire universe.

Our Naked Souls

My soul
Unfolded before you
Like a flower's petals.

Naked and unhidden,
I kept nothing from you.
And though I was afraid
You would think less of me,
I held nothing back.

It was the feeling of light
Hitting places
Once withered by darkness.

You held me gently
As I was vulnerable.
You looked at my flaws
And saw beauty
Where I only saw defects.

We stood there together,
Our naked souls
Affirming an eternal love.
Nothing hidden, all laid bare—
Together, you and I
Are finally free.

Certain

I will wait
As long as it takes
For our paths
To cross
In just the right way.

I will wait
With unrelenting certainty
That you are the one,
The other half of me.

I am certain
That we
Are meant
For each other.

The Chessboard

I've been hurt before.
I've put my heart
In careless hands
And paid for it.

I'm defensive.
I learned my lesson
Never to trust too much
Or else be hurt again.

I'm paranoid.
I feel like I need to be
One step ahead
Of everyone else
Or I won't be ready
When betrayal
Inevitably comes.

I'm afraid
That if I don't play the game
Better than anyone else
Then I'll lose—
Checkmate.

But she would never do that
To me.

Because she's not my opponent;
She's on my side.
For the first time
I'm not alone
Against the world
And I need
To remember that.

Complacency

It's important not to get complacent.
Once we've been happy for a long while,
It's easy to see tiny things as issues
That we would've never cared about before.

We forget that we are loved
And we moan about mole-hills
From the peaks of mountains.
It's all too easy
To get tunnel vision
And lose the bigger picture.

Hold on tightly to your remembrance
Of the incomparable gift of love;
Never forget how your joy
Has bloomed from the roots of sorrow
Under the nourishment of her light—

Love is remembering what you have.

Eternal

When time has run its course
And all the symphonies,
All the great paintings,
And all the films
Have been created
And worn down to dust,

Still our love will remain
Etched in the cosmos
As if by the hand of god.

Kintsugi Heart

Every past heartbreak
Was just a lesson
Teaching me how to love you better.

Instead of hiding our broken hearts,
Let us fill the cracks with gold
And put them on display for all to see.

Do not conceal the pain
That made you who you are today—
Wear it proudly.

Find someone
Who looks at the places
Your heart has been broken
And sees a place to love you better,
Sees beauty where others see flaws.

Oasis

You were my oasis
In the desert.

When I felt hopeless
You made me whole.

Yourself

I love the way
You are yourself
So effortlessly
With no need
To pretend
Or hold back.

You rise like the sun
Full of confidence,
Certain of your place
In the universe,
And unafraid of the opinions
Of others.

Wasted Moments

I must live with the remorse
Of every moment
I did not spend kissing your lips
For it was all wasted time.

Experiences are meant
To be shared,
And life not
Too carefully planned.

I wish I'd
Thrown caution to the wind,
Giving you all I had,
Building palaces from dirt mounds.

Conversations, souls in abandon
Yearning to be free,
Tugging at the chains of conformity,
Deciding our fates for ourselves.

Chapter Two

Broken Hearts

Foreboding

Though we thought it would last forever
It seems our hearts had other plans.
They began to withdraw from one another
Far before we did.

The Forest

Do you feel the moss under your hands?
Do you smell the forest air?
Do you see the sun through the trees
And hear the birds singing?

We have met here many times
In my mind:
The forest behind that old house
Where I escaped to so often.

Do you remember this place?
We have been here together, you know,
More times than I can count.
This is where I keep my love for you.

This is where I keep you contained,
A fantasy that can never come true.
This is where I feel most free.
This is the well of unmade memories.

The Worst Lie

The worst lie
Our culture teaches us
Is that romantic love
Is the answer
To all of life's problems,

As if it is some magic spell
That suddenly transforms life
Into a rose-colored wonderland
Without struggle or pain.

The Same Old Path

These days my mind wanders
Toward you
Far more often
Than I would like.

I can't stop thinking about you;
You take up space
I should be using
For more pressing matters.

I retread the same path
As if visiting the same place
Over and over again
Could lead to a different result.

Cast Off the Remnants

Everything was in slow motion
As I unclenched my hand
And released yours from my grasp.

We were alone, floating in the middle
Of a dark chasm.
Your face recoiled
As you realized
You could no longer use me.

Instantly a weight lifted from my chest
And I was free
As I cast off the remnants
Of the person
You forced me to become.

Finally I burst from my shell,
On the verge of death,
Gasping for air.

I am free, free
Reaching for the heavens.
I am free, free
Taking my life
Back into my hands.

The Thought of Losing You

I struggle with the thought of losing you.
What would I be
Without you?
I want to hold you tight
And cherish the feeling of you
And your warmth next to me.

But I know I can't hold on too tightly
Because that's how flames are smothered
And that's how romance dies.

Before, it was only a dream
That our love could blossom
Into something special.
But now that my dream has come true
Fear of loss grips me.

I have to accept that I can't control life
And I must live in the moment,
Cherishing your every detail
While I still have you.

For as long as I get to love you
I will love you with all that I am.

Sunlight

Addicted
To the idea
Of love,

We were like seeds
Which sat in the sun
Expecting to grow
But withering away,

Forgetting the value
Of soil and rain.

If I Should Lose You

If I should lose you,
I want you to know
That I will never truly
Get over you.

You gave me everything I could want
And I tried to do the same,
Though that wasn't much.

If I should lose you,
Know that I only want you
To be happy,
That I only wish you the best.
And if that means
You must love someone else,
Then so be it,
Because I love you
More than I love myself.
And if I have to suffer every day
Watching you love a better man,
Then I will put on a smiling mask
And be happy for you.

If I should lose you,
Know that I lost everything.

Liars

I have seen what people will do
Just to keep loneliness at bay.
They will fake whole relationships
And lie about their intentions
Just because they cannot stand
To be alone with themselves.

Maze

I am afraid
That I am wasting
My one chance
To be truly honest
With myself.

Am I chasing after whispers?
You tell me they will slip through my hands
Like some vacant apparition;
Perhaps you are right,
And my belief that I
Might someday catch them
Is only self-indulgence. . . .

Maybe I'm throwing away
The best thing in my life
For reasons that don't make sense.

You make it so easy to doubt myself:
Because it was never all bad,
I don't feel like I'm allowed to leave,
That I'm being selfish,
That I owe you something.

I'm afraid I've gotten lost
In a maze of my own making.

Blacksmith

I pour my heart out on these pages.
Ruthlessly I melt it down
Like molten gold
And pound it into shape
With my pen.

Why do I do this to myself?
What do I have to gain
By causing myself
To relive the same pain?

Remorse

I didn't think
The small moments
Would be so difficult—

Seeing something funny
And wanting to share it with you
As I always do

But then remembering
Our unbroken silence.
Waves of remorse overtake me.

Train in the Night

I lie awake in my bed,
Listening to the sound
Of the train passing by
In the night.

It reminds me
Of our careless adventures,
Untethered to earthly demands,
Free of constraints.

It's all I can do to stop myself
From packing my bags
And leaving this place
As quickly as I can.

Too many memories here,
Too many forlorn ghosts
Reminding me of a happiness
That has long since passed.

Derelict Castles

We built a castle together
On a hill near the sea.

I hate to see it derelict
With no one to tend the grounds.

I thought it would be better
If we ended things peacefully,

But now I think it might be worse
To see what we built still standing,
Just abandoned, but not broken down.
Perhaps it would be better off as ashes.

Horcruxes

These photos—
So many horcruxes
Containing the soul
Of us,

Our unforgivable sin,
The murder we committed
Together.

We are each haunted
By the specter of the deed,
Or at least I am.
And if I must bear this pain
I hope you feel it, too.

Leaving

The hardest lesson of heartbreak
Is that you can still love someone
While knowing you shouldn't be with them.

That makes it all the harder to let go,
All the harder to be the one who leaves,
All the harder to abandon ship.

Captive

I find myself wanting
To cleanse my mind
Of your memory.

If I could just forget
The magic of your touch
And the rush that accompanied
Your every word,

Perhaps then I could be free.

I am a prisoner
Of your memory,
A captive
Of possibility,

But every day I inch closer
To leaving you in the past.

You may break my heart
But you cannot lock my soul away.

Erosion

All of our small memories
Will be forgotten
As time erodes their edges
As surely as the sea
Erodes the shore,
Until all that is left of us
Is a vague remembrance
Of what used to be everything.

Echoes

I stumble upon
An old photograph of us
That transports me
To the place we used to be.

I hear the echoes
Of our joyous laughter;
Our journey passes me by
Like a rock skipped onto a wave.

The memory ejects me
And I return to the present,
Reminded of how
Life turned joy into misery.

Changed Locks

You never deserved what I gave you.
You saw my love as an opportunity.
You came and went as you pleased.
I hate to say it, but you used me.

Next time you come around
You will find that the locks have changed
And your key no longer works.

You will find that I've changed my number
And your voicemails will remain unanswered.
Though I doubt you'd bother sending any,
Still, I will never check

This is the closure I deserve.

Someone

You didn't care
Who you were kissing—
You just wanted to be kissed.

You didn't care
Who you were loving—
You just wanted to be loved.

You didn't care,
You just wanted someone;
You didn't care if it was me.

Bittersweet Mistake

Driving around these empty streets
In the middle of the night,
Wondering if this was all
Some bittersweet mistake.

The problem with love
Is that it's not so easy to tell
Where the good ends and the bad begins.
They don't separate like oil and water;
The difference isn't clear—
Everything is muddled.

I don't know if it's worth it
To keep fighting
For what we have.
I don't know
Where these streets
Will take me.

Justin Wetch

Your Favorite Place

The vines cascade down
Over the whitewashed brick.
The avant-garde décor
Clashes with the patrons:
The place you always loved.
Now I'm here alone
And I can finally say
How much I hate it.

How a toddler
Could make better coffee,
How a craft aisle
Has more class,
How . . .

How much I miss you,
If I'm being honest.

87

Out in the Rain

I hope you find someone
Who gives you the feeling
Of completeness
You were always looking for.

I hope you find someone
Who would rather
Stay inside when it rains
Than go out into it.

I hope you find someone
Who gives you everything
You ever wanted
That I couldn't.

Expendable

It is such a painful realization
To see that you
Never loved me
For who I was.

You only loved me
For the place I could hold
In your life
Whenever you found it convenient.

To you I was expendable,
Just another listening ear
And comforting voice.

Tell me, did it ever dawn on you
That our conversations
Would be no different
If I were anyone else?

I wish you cared about me
And not just
What I did for you.

Soften the Blow

I spent far too long
Wondering how to do it
Without making it my fault.

I think I would've hurt you less
If I had just told you I was unhappy
Instead of trying to soften the blow.

Prisoner

It took me far too long
To realize
That by indulging in the pain
Every time I thought about you,

I built these altars,
These shrines of rose-colored memories,
To worship the thought of you.

Perhaps I took comfort in the familiarity
And became a willing prisoner
Of my self-inflicted misery.

It took me far too long
To realize
I should've celebrated,
Rather than mourned,
The death of us.

A Place I Cannot Go

There's another universe
Somewhere out there
Where we
Are still together.

It breaks my heart
That it exists
Yet I can never go there.

If only I could jump in a spaceship
And fly through the multiverse
To find that happy place.

If only it were that simple;
If only I could run away
To that place
I cannot go.

Harmony

I miss sharing the moments with you.
I miss the feeling
Of experiencing life
With someone else.

Watching you enjoy a sunset
Was like poetry,
Music became spiritual,
And food became art.

Without you
The sun still sets,
Food still nourishes,
And there is still music—
But it is dissonant.

You were the harmony,
The synthesis of melodies
Into something greater.

Without you
The music feels
Dull.

Cut Away

I let you cut away
At my identity
Piece by piece
Until I could hardly
Recognize myself.

By giving up
Parts of myself
To make you happy,
I made myself miserable.

That is a mistake
I will never make
Again.

Moving Away

Sometimes I think
Of packing up my bags
And moving
To Los Angeles
Like every other artist
Trying to find
Some sense of belonging.

Sometimes I think
Of flying off to New York,
As if the city lights
Could somehow
Hold back the darkness.

Sometimes I think
Of getting a van
And driving down
The coast,
Hoping that experiences
Could chip away
At my uncertainty.

But I know none of that would work:
Changing the scenery
Does not change the soul.

A Ship Without an Anchor

You can't let love
Define your life.

If you need another person
To validate you
For who you are,
You become a ship
Without an anchor
That can float from
Harbor to harbor

But can never moor
On solid ground.

Tides

I can't keep letting myself
Fall back in love with you
Over and over again;
I can't tie my heart
To the ups and downs
Of your waves.

You make me happier
Than anyone ever has.
You bring me to the crests
Of mountainous ocean waves,
Tasting Elysium in the wind.

But when you are done
Playing with me,
I fall down, plunging.
I keep forgetting how much
It hurts to fall
From such a great height.

I have been wounded
Too many times before.
It's time I learned my lesson—
I cannot afford to tie my heart
To the ups and downs of someone
Who doesn't care enough to be careful.

Broad Strokes

The curse of time is that we
Are no longer entranced
By the magic of moments;
As dry history replaces vivid art
And details we didn't notice
Replace the broad strokes
We first fell in love with.

Half-Hearted

I'll always treasure the moments we had
But in truth I don't know
If I will ever love again,
At least not with my whole heart,
Because part of it
Will always be yours.

Sober Love

When was the last time we just . . . hung out? Spent time together? Sober. Clean. It's been so long, I don't even remember. . . . What if we've forgotten how to love the real versions of each other? What if our brains are so fucked up, they'll love anything? I just want to know. Give me a night with you, the real you. Let me touch you and kiss you and love you—I just want to feel again. I want to be together in that wretched sobriety, that dullness, and remember the way it was when we first fell in love.

Utopia

We are consumed
With being in love.
We hold up romance
As some kind of utopia—
If only we could make it there,
All our problems
All our sorrows
All our pain
All our suffering
Would be dispelled by the power
Of love
As if by magic.

But that's not how life works.

There is no utopia,
No magical solution.
Love cannot fix us
No matter how much we wish
It could.

Dystopia

Broken glasses, cloudy vision,
Dust and haze hangs in the air,
Half-decimated skyscrapers on either side
Of this bleak, deserted highway.

This is a trip down memory lane,
As I must return here now and again
And look upon the desolate ruins
Of the world we built together.

I am only a tourist here these days
And I see it with calmer eyes now,
No longer shocked by the destruction
The way I used to be.

Time has calmed my spirit
And made still the rivers of grief.
Soon, I am sure, this once-grand city
Will be a forgotten speck on an ancient map.

Milestones

The first time I saw her
I felt it in my face
As I smiled.

The first time we kissed
I felt it in my spine
As if it were lightning.

When I first told her I loved her,
I felt it in my chest
As nervousness took away my breath.

The first time we fought
I felt it in my stomach
As regret made me nauseous.

When it ended,
I felt nothing
At first,

Before I felt
It all
At once.

Burnt Matches

Every time we try
To rekindle
This same old match
It only burns deeper
Into the fabric
Of who I am
Until there's nothing left
Of me
But ash.

It's so tempting
To feel the spark
One last time.

But each time
Hurts more,
And each time
Less and less of me
Remains.

Limitless

Young and in love,
We walked the street
As the cool autumn air
Gently touched our faces.

Optimistic, unacquainted with failure,
We saw only possibility
Instead of limitations.

If only we
Could have stayed
That way.

Selfish

It's not selfish
To do what makes you happy.

You don't owe anyone
Anything.

Let no one lay claim to your life
To use for their own happiness.

You are your own person;
You must put yourself first.

Wind

You shattered my heart
Into a thousand tiny fragments
And tossed them to the wind
Without a care.

Explanations

I have always felt
That I owe everyone
An explanation
For everything.

You see, this is why
I have the right
To be the way
That I am
Or do
What I am doing.

But I am done giving
Explanations.

I don't owe you
Anything.

Not a damn thing.

Unending War

There is an unending war
Between my intuition and my heart.
They want opposite things:
To love you or leave you forever.

I am afraid there will never be peace
Until it is already too late,
Until this conflict has destroyed
Any chances of moving on.

Relief

When those words left my mouth
Like bullets from a gun,
I thought the recoil would hurt me
As much as it hurt you.

I thought the world would crumble around me
And I would be awash with remorse,
Having to fight to keep strong,
Surviving in some great struggle

But the words slipped out by accident
And I didn't feel destroyed;
All I felt
Was relief.

Embrace Your Madness

Do not let go of the chaos
That wraps itself around your soul.
Do not let the world tame you
When your spirit yearns to be free.
Embrace the madness within you
That defies the decrees of monotony.
Do not let the world cloud your light;
Do not let the world chip away
At the infinity within you.

Endless Ink

You are a bottomless well
Of pain to me.

No matter how many times
I dip my pen
Into the ink
Of us

It never runs dry.

I don't know how it's possible
To love
—and yet hate—
Someone
So much.

Sandcastles

I am prone to thinking
That the relationships we build
Will be permanent by default,
Standing strong against time,
Only building upward.

But relationships aren't stone manors;
They're sandcastles on the beach,
Modeled after the real thing,
But which only wash away
With the next tide,
Weak and immaterial,
As ephemeral as a smell
Or an idea.

Looking at You

I look at you
And instantly
Every scenario
That could have been
Springs to mind.

My soul is crushed
As I look at the space
Between us;
We could be standing closer,
Happy and in love
But not in this life.

No, in this life
I will forever be haunted
By everything
We could have been.

I would give up anything
In life
To have you.

Love Does Not Subtract

The most important thing
I have learned
From relationships
Is that you should never settle
For someone
Who makes you feel
Like you need to be
Less of yourself
To please them.

Be with someone
Who pushes you
To become
More and more
Of who
You are meant to be.

High-Rise View

I have spent so much time
Being heartbroken
Over people
Who were never really mine
To begin with.

I get attached too quickly
To grandiose ideas
Of everything we could be.

I never seem to learn
That foundations take time,
And I am far too anxious
To jump to the high-rise view
Without actually building that tall.

Justin Wetch

The Second Loss

I don't know
Which hurt worse,

When I first lost you
Or when the memories
Began to lose their color
And the feelings
Began to lose their passion.

The pain of heartbreak
Is always twofold:
First, you lose them
And then you lose
The parts of yourself
That loved them.

Alternate Endings

I never told you how I felt about you.
I never told you I loved you.
I never told you what you meant to me.
I never told you the truth.

You carry pieces of my soul
No one else has ever seen.
Tell me, do you treasure them?
Or have you already let them go?

These alternate endings
Dangle in my hands
Like loose strings.

These are the remnants
Of all the stories
Never finished.

Growing a Rose

I have been guilty
Of falling too fast
And too hard.

I have expected rosebuds
Before the stem
Was strong enough
To support them.

I never learned to take it slowly
To build with care and caution
But so it is with youthful love.

Our Bridge

I find myself regretting the way
I burned down our bridge
With such reckless anger.

I find myself sitting
At the edge of the cliff,
The sea that separates us
Stretching out before me.

I imagine that you are sitting too
At the place where our bridge
Once connected
The lands of our souls.

Do you mourn for us like I do?
Are you as obsessed as I am
With all the different ways
Our story could've ended?

But there's no use sitting here
Much longer.
Hope alone could not restore
What we once had.

It's time I moved on.

Mature Endings

I want the type of relationship
Where we wouldn't feel the need
To delete the pictures
If it ended.

I want to catch up
Every once in a while
Over coffee
And accept that it stopped working
But be grateful for when it did.

I want to know
That if it ends,
It was despite our best efforts
And best intentions.

Know that if it ends
I will never speak badly of you
Or what we built together.

And even if
The time comes
To stop
Loving you,

I will never stop loving you.

Chapter Three

Weary Spirits

Burns

It burns
Like acid
On exposed skin.

The world manifests its joy
In displays of grandeur,
Laughing at me
While holding me at a distance.

I built a magnificent castle,
Laying brick by brick by brick
Against miles of meadows
And perfectly-trimmed hedges.

But I am its sole occupant,
And no one else
Has ever bothered
To come see it.

And so it will decay
With my body,
Becoming nothing more than a curiosity
For archaeologists of the future.

Depression, it burns
Like acid on exposed skin.

The Desert

The desert stretches out
As far as I can see
In every direction.

The horizon
Blurs into oblivion—
There is no escape.

I am parched beyond measure;
My skin boils under the heat
Of a relentless sun.

I cannot die,
Though I wish I could
And bring an end to all this.

Though I run in one direction
With cracked bones
Piercing through paper-like skin.

I can never escape it,
Doomed
To keep running,

No respite, no end,
The panic goes on.

Justin Wetch

True Strength

They say
You will never face
A struggle
More powerful
Than you can take.

They're wrong.

There will be many times
In your life
When you come up against things
That you cannot overcome.

And that's okay.

True strength is not
Trying to be stronger
Than anything that may come.

True strength is being willing
To admit
That you
Are not strong enough
On your own.

The Easy Way Out

Some say medication is the easy way out.
They think that if you just
Do enough yoga,
Drink enough tea,
Or smoke enough weed,
Then somehow this mental mess
Will be magically cured
And the tides
Of imbalanced chemicals
Will somehow shift
Into proper form
And there will be peace
At last. . . .

If only that were true.

I'm not ashamed
To say I took the "easy way out,"
Because this is not a battle
I can win on my own
And there is so much serenity
In admitting that.

I took the easy way out
Because I am not strong enough
On my own.

The Uncertain Road

Life doesn't come with an instruction manual.

Admitting this evokes fear.
Uncertainty. Possibility of failure. Difficulty.
The road is dark and full of obstacles.

Life doesn't come with an instruction manual.

But this is liberating.
Uncertainty becomes adventure;
Possible failure makes success all the sweeter—
Difficulty makes it more rewarding

Life doesn't come with an instruction manual.

Although it is fraught with peril, life's
Uncertainty, once accepted, becomes
Its greatest source of joy and happiness.

The Train of Thought

Suddenly I am ahead of it,
Questioning its direction,
Confused, thinking that these
Ideas don't quite sound like me.

I think it's happening again.
I wish I were strong enough
To will this planet
To stop spinning so quickly.

I am glued in place,
Powerless to move,
In denial that this panic
Belongs to me.

I thought I was doing better
But stability does not love me back.
I hate how powerless I am
Over my own mind.

Whirl of Chaos

The day flies past
In a whirl of chaos
Flashing by
All too quickly.

Trying to slow down
And find a moment
Of peace
Feels as impossible
As stopping
The rotation of the earth
With my own two hands.

The Offer of Escape

We dance every night, you and I,
Long past the midnight hour.
Though we never touch
The temptation is always there.

Escape.

Your promises are too good to be true.
You say freedom is just a touch away
And there will be no consequences for me;
The last page will turn, the story complete.

Temptation.

Your hand, outstretched to me,
Begging for my surrender—
But for one more night, at least,
I resist, and the game starts over.

Demons

As a kid I was told
That mental illness
Is just the result of demons
Inhabiting the body.

I was taught
That if I just prayed hard enough,
I would be set free.

Those demons
Still follow me today—
Years of suffering,
Thinking it was all my fault
For not believing hard enough
—Some scars that may never heal.

Grasping

Peace,
Elusive
As grasping
For the wind.

It moves here and there
No matter how hard you try;
You cannot take it
In your hands.

All you can do
Is sit still,
Give up all delusions
Of control,
And let peace
Find you
Where you are.

Simple Life

I wonder whether that simple life
I see walking down the street
Would make me happy.

That man with his wife
Walking with their young son—
They look so peaceful together.

I feel so lost in what I want
I do not know what life I desire
Or where it would lead me.

Writer's Block

The pen aches to write
But the mind
Is a barren wasteland.

The soul begs to erupt
With feeling and passion
But only ash coughs out.

The heart is illiterate
Yet desperate to be understood
Scribbling nonsensical symbols.

Justin Wetch

Could Have Been

The could-have-been
Of our story
Is what really hurts.

At least if we had tried and failed,
There would be closure
And that road would be clearly marked
As a dead end.

But there is no catharsis,
Only mixed feelings—
What-ifs and I-wishes.

And we will die wondering
What we could have built
Together
If we'd tried.

Salt in the Wind

Purpose. Destiny. Calling. Meaning.

I tasted just a hint of them
In the salty air by the sea,
Coming back to this place
I had not visited
In so many years.

It was like I could feel
Who I was
The last time I was here,

And suddenly I was filled
With the most bitter remorse
Over what I had become since then:

A man hunting after shadows
Of the convictions that used to
Overflow.

Fighter

You have fought your way
Through deserts and jungles,
Pressing water from the leaves,
Wrapping bloody feet
With makeshift bandages.

You have fought
Your way through life,
Not out of desire
But necessity.

I am proud of how far
You have managed to come
Despite your challenges.

One day I wish to see you
Lay down your weapons
And find solace in peace.

Bloody

They trampled over the masses
On their way to greater riches
Not even bothering
To clean the blood off their shoes.

Freedom

Forced to be crushed under the heel
Of exploitative masters
Is not freedom.

Being free to choose
Which insurance company screws you
Is not freedom.

Being free to choose death
Over medical bankruptcy
Is not freedom.

Being free to choose between
Exploitation and starvation
Is not freedom.

We need to pay more attention
To the price of freedom;
It is rising.

Poison

They will never understand the effort it takes people like us just to get up in the morning, to face the day as if the very thought of it doesn't crush us.

They will never understand the way it feels to worry about and question every aspect of your life, to have the precious moments poisoned by insecurity. They will never understand, and that makes it all the more difficult because ignorance leads to resentment, and our fear of being resented only leads to more anxiety.

To us, drinking poison is a daily ritual. It just hurts all the more coming from those we love.

Trust Issues

Understand that I may never quite believe you when you tell me you love me, and I may never trust that the sun will come up again the next morning even though I have seen it thousands of times before.

Understand that no matter how much I love you, there will always be a part of me that is so afraid of being hurt that it is always vigilant, waiting for the first sign of confirmation that I am as unlovable as I always suspected.

Understand that though I am damaged and weary from battles lost, I will never stop fighting for you and your happiness, no matter what it costs me.

First Draft

I am often so concerned with creating something perfect on the first try that I do not try to create something new at all out of fear of failure. I have this ingrained idea, which will not loosen no matter how hard I try, that I cannot be seen as unfinished in any aspect. That is why this time—

Unuttered Words

I keep this secret book
Of unuttered words
Locked away
In the recesses
Of my soul.

Shrouded in darkness,
Its every page
Is scarred with memories
And untold truths.

I think each one of them
Will follow me to the grave
As if they never existed.

Sad in Paradise

You can be sad in paradise too, you know.

I thought
That if I flew away
And escaped my troubles
On the beaches
Of this beautiful island,
Then I would leave
My sadness behind
And feel
New.

But it was not to be.

No change of scenery
Can change what's inside of you;
The battle follows us everywhere—
There is no solace, no rest.

Memento Mori

Hold death always before your eyes;
Let it cast its long shadow over your sunny days.
For though we transmute stone into power,
Our ingenuity cloaking us in the powers of gods,
Though we beat back our mortality
With modern medicine and technology,
Still death is patient,
Creeping slowly toward us
As the decades flow by.
Each one of us meets our end
In our due time.

But death is only a mirror.
Death is a teacher, a friend
Allowing us to know
The importance of the present.
Mortality is solace.

Kings and Queens of Bridges Burned

We were king and queen
Of the ashes,
Of every bridge we burned
Leading back to our pasts.

We forsook the easy answers,
Finding solace in broken mirrors,
The ambiguity of this road of ours
Leading neither here nor there.

To See the Stars

Stasis is comfortable.
It asks nothing of us.
But at some point
You have to ask yourself
If you'd rather
Stay comfortable
And never climb the mountain
To see the stars.

Tempered by Pain

Iron cannot become steel
Without going through the fire.

And so it is the same
With you
And the hard times
In your life.

You cannot become your best self
Without being tempered by pain.

Justin Wetch

A Fistful of Sand in the Wind

Life just won't slow down
Though I plant my feet
Firmly on the ground.
It seems
That the seconds keep getting shorter
And life flies
Ever more quickly
Out of my hands,
Like a fistful of sand
Held in the wind.

Before too long
Life will pass me by.

I fear that it will feel
Empty and unloved,
Merely a blur,
The days and years
Coalescing
Into mundane gray.

Flashbacks

The most random things
Trigger old memories.

They drift into the present,
Tangled strings
Linking the then and the now
Like ships' anchors
Which never found
The ocean's floor.

The times are so different
And I often wonder
Whether they can possibly be real.
It doesn't make sense
That all of these colored moments
Can coexist.

I yearn
For a time that never existed,
When all of this made sense.

The 28th of February

The worst night of my life
Was the 28th of February.
It started off as a simple evening
Hanging out with friends
But became a panic attack
That never seemed to end.

I asked my friends to leave;
It seemed like their every word
Stretched out for a thousand years.
Everything turned to wax,
My heart rate was a machine gun,
And I could barely breathe,
Stuck in a moment of complete fear.

I had to go to the emergency room;
The walls were closing in on me.
Friendly faces were unrecognizable.
Nothing would hold still.
I was gone.
It hurt too much to bear:
My confidence splintered,
My sense of self forever damaged—
That night never ended;
No, it stays with me still.

Every Breath a Battle

You live many lives,
Most of them
At war
With one another.

That is the nature
Of human existence;

We can never be truly happy
Because we are not capable
Of accepting our lives
Without wondering
What could have been,

And there remains part of each of us
That wants a different outcome.

And we wish we could drown
The defectors within ourselves
And silence their voices
Forevermore.

And so we are left
With a happiness
That can never be
Complete.

Anxious

I have heard so many people
Say that anxiety is silly,
But they don't know what it feels like
To have a mind
Constantly at war with itself,
Constantly fighting an endless battle
Where all you ever do is lose.

They don't know what it feels like
To not be able to enjoy life
Without second-guessing your place
In anything and everything.

You can no more
Defeat your own anxiety
Than you can will your heart to stop beating.

Triumph

We are not
A collection of failures
Because of the things
We did not win.

We are a collection of triumphs,
A middle finger raised high
Against the forces in life
That wanted to see us stay down.

We are triumphant
Because we kept fighting
Even when it seemed
Like all was lost.

Justin Wetch

Hues of Melancholy

There it is. The feeling of being alone. It's been a while, but I remember you. Yes, I've been happy for a while now, but god knows that never lasts, and I had almost forgotten your memory. But there it is, that frigid, icy-blue sadness. I can't ever escape you for long, can I? I can't even be happy without tasting you in the back of my mouth, knowing it'll end and soon you'll consume my every sense. Your scent lingers like a strong cologne, coloring even my brightest moments with hues of melancholy. There is no freedom—there is only this. And here I am, again . . . alone.

Vrai

It was real. It was all real.
As real as anything has ever been
Or ever seemed to be:

The night's sky ebbed
Into a pool of ink.
I was falling
Endlessly downward,
Unable to breathe.

At long last I gave up
And the liquid filled my lungs,
Leaking into my veins.

Suddenly I was weightless,
Floating among the stars,
Unchained from the gravity
Of the earth.

Conflicting Desires

I hope you read this
And know
How I really feel about you.

I hope you never read this
And never know
How I really feel about you.

Final

We fool ourselves into thinking
That we are afraid of the unknown,
Of the meaning of life,
When truthfully
We have known all along
And are just too afraid
To admit it:

There is no higher meaning,
There is no greater purpose,
There is no transcendence—
Death is final.

But that is not something
To be afraid of;
It's something
To embrace.
Both the magnificent and the macabre,
The glorious and the grotesque.

Not in This Life

Life disappears in a blink
And suddenly it's over,
Dreams dormant and unfulfilled,
Our minds a collection
Of could-have-beens.

Perhaps it would've been better
To never know of the stars
And have a soul desperate to touch them
Than to have known of them,
All too aware
That they could never be touched.

At least, not in this life.

The Winding Road

I don't know if these confusing and winding roads will
someday lead to the place I need to be. I can only hope
that one day, as I look in the rearview mirror, I will
be able to see that this was all guiding me toward my
destiny. I can only hope that this serpentine road will
someday make sense, and all of my struggles will add up
to something worth it.

Ocean

The mind is an ocean;
The surface ripples
With chaotic energy,
But deep down
In the endless depths
There is a stillness,
Seemingly outside of time.
There is nothing
In all directions,

Only the feeling
Of floating
In the silence.

Find this place
In your moments of stress;
Find the peace
Of the depths.

Our Dreams

I remember people by their dreams,
By their hopes and fears;

I hold on to these strings of the soul
Because surface details change:
Hair turns gray
And memories fade.

But the bare nakedness of a person,
Their deepest core
That has burned with desire
Since it was formed of stardust
Eons ago,

These things are more a person
Than the disposable husks
We call bodies.

These things rage on,
Giving us purpose and life,
For it is our dreams
That burn our fingerprints
Into the fabric of the universe.

It is our dreams that make us immortal.

Justin Wetch

The Way Things Used to Look

It seems to me that the atmosphere of life
Feels distinctly different from time to time.
Our memories are tinged with the colors
Of its hues and vibrancy.

I feel, for instance,
That the summers of my youth
Were so much more red and yellow
Than the colors of the moment.

They were infected with optimism,
Permeated with a carefree lightness,
Everything airy and warm,
Unaware of seeing the future.

The cold of an early spring
Prickles the hairs on the back of my neck
Even now, even now
Just in remembrance of it.

As I came of age: the dull, muted green
That colored all things
And the golden, glowing radiance
Of a time only remembered in shadows.

Weary Spirits

Place your weary spirit
Between my arms.
Lonely as it may be,
We are less alone
Against this cold world
When we hold each other:
Two weary spirits
Finding a little warmth
Together.

Breaking the Cycle

"I want a divorce," she said to him, dropping the papers on the table that were already bearing her signature. "What?" he replied. "I'm not fucking signing that." I watched, peeking out from around the corner, grasping the faded paint of that wall with my small hands, wondering if this meant a future of two half-families. I turned away and ran to my room, pushing away the end of this story like a horror movie you just can't finish. I'll never threaten someone I love with something so awful, I promised myself. I'll never treat someone like this; I'll never be like either of them; I'll find my own path. I'll never be like them. The shouting was so loud that night that I ran to the edge of our three acres of forest and still couldn't escape the noises echoing across the landscape like shells obliterating a battlefield. I covered my ears, and still the muffled sounds broke through.

We are not destined to relive the sins of our fathers. The mistakes of those who came before us are not written into our DNA. The choice to transcend rather than imitate remains ours.

I am not them. I will never act like them. I am my own, and I will not hurt others the way I was hurt.

Life Is Precious

Life is far too
Precious a gift to
Waste.

Our time on this earth
Is a mere blink.

And yet this is
Paradoxical:
As we seek to
Skim the cream
From the best of
Life,

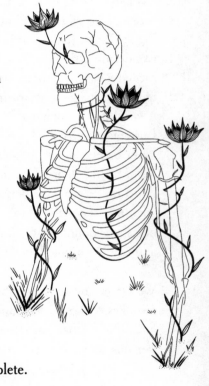

We neglect
Everything else,

The smaller things
That make it
Feel all the more complete.

The Raging River

Now that the current
Of that raging river
Has been dammed up,

Now that the waves
No longer coalesce
Into violent swells,

I don't miss the chaos
The way I thought
I would.

I find joy in the balance,
And rest in the serenity
Of peace at last.

Here is love without jealousy,
Passion without anger,
And hope without anxiety.

The monsoons have subsided,
The seasons have changed,
And I'm all the better for it.

Chapter Four

Cosmic

Minds

Chance

Created by chance,
We dance in the flames,
Our existence uncertain,
Our place among the stars
Hanging by a thread.

Looking up at the cosmos,
We wonder:
If we blink the wrong way,
Would it all vanish in an instant?

You Were Always Like That

I think about the way you would lean over me to stare out the plane window if you were here with me. You would give the beautiful city lights, set against the vast sea of darkness, all of the attention they deserve, enjoying it this time as much as if it were your first. You were always like that, you know. Hungry to devour all of the small gifts life offered. You were not the type to sit back, jaded and exasperated by any kind of experience. Even the remarkable duality of soaring through the air unrestrained by the bounds of the earth, set against the drudgery of the human beings packed like sardines in a tin can, could not dampen your spirit.

It's times like these when I miss you the most.

Projection

To create art
Is to project your soul
Into the physical world,
To be seen and judged by all,

Open and vulnerable.
Art has the audacity
To proclaim,
"I have the right
To be who I am."

Nostalgia

They will romanticize us,
Yearning for the supposed simplicity of our time,
Mythologizing our artists and musicians, our philoso-
phers,
Adoring the way we see the world
As if we were not human beings just like them,
Fallible and uncertain,
Making it up as we went along.

Ode to Silence

I have had quite enough of music;
Every song begins to sound the same.

Instead I prefer the music of silence,
Which is always the same, yet always feels different.

There is the silence of the morning
With the freshness of rain just past,

There is the silence near the sea
Colored bluish green like the water,

There is the silence of a sunny day
Cascading down with gentle joy,

And there is the silence of the night
Which hushes creation into slumber.

Among all these silences, the most beautiful
Is the one within your own soul,

Which makes all the other silences
Much more beautiful still.

Summation

We are not merely the sum of our
Sunsets and sunrises.

We are not the math of the rotations
Of planets, moons, and stars.

The pacing of mankind's calendar
Is not the thudding heartbeat
Of your story.

We can be free of the iron shackles
Of patterns that dictate our lives.

We are alive, we are free, we are
Human.

Justin Wetch

A Beautiful Abstraction

What a beautiful abstraction, music is.
It serves no purpose for our survival,
And yet, here it is;
It transcends utility,
Existing for the sake of its beauty.

Music proves to us
That life can be more
Than survival.

Talking About the Weather

Someone once told me
That interesting people
Don't talk about the weather,
But I don't think that's
Quite true.

It is the most
Interesting topic of all
Because no one is ever
Talking about the weather
When they
Talk about the weather.

A husband and wife are walking in a park.
"I want to save our marriage,"
He says with a "Nice day, isn't it?"
"Too late—my heart has moved on,"
She says with a nod and "Uh huh."

An old couple sits together on a bench.
"If it ends today, it was worth it with you,"
She says with a "Cold out, isn't it?"
"I have no regrets, not a single one,"
He says with a "Here, take my jacket."

Sometimes the most beautiful gems
Are buried deep in ordinary-looking rocks
Disguised with many others
On an ocean shore
Stretching miles in the distance.

Sometimes the most beautiful I-love-yous
Are buried in ordinary conversation
And disguised as trivial comments.

Tell me you love me,
Show me you care,
Come talk about the weather.

The Purpose of Poetry

What is the purpose of poetry?

If it is merely self-expression,
It is literary self-indulgence
And the reader is unnecessary;

If it is to comfort the reader,
Then it becomes little more
Than empty pandering;

If it is to be relatable,
It must be watered down
Into vague clichés.

What, then,
Is the purpose of poetry?

I think perhaps
Poetry exists
To rise above function
And elevate the sights of our souls
Beyond the horizon
Toward hope.

Rain

We are engaged in a glorious collaboration,
You and I,
The author and the reader.

If a poem calls for rain, and I write it so,
It does not rain unless you allow it.

If I intend the rain to cleanse the soul
But you are a flower in thirst of rain,
Then together we have created
Something different—

A moment that belongs to the two of us alone,
For no two readings are the same.

Infinite Worlds

There are so many worlds
That exist in the universes
Of our minds.

We could never travel to all of them
And learn their secrets
Even if we had many lifetimes to do so.

According to multiverse theory
Every possible universe
Exists—
Every fictional world
Thought up by brilliant writers
Actually exists
In reality.

I like to imagine
That writers don't create these worlds—
We merely discover them
As the ethereal tendrils of our minds
Reach across universes.

By the same token
Every dream and nightmare
We've ever had
Is also a real world;
Perhaps our minds are like televisions
Flipping through universes like channels
Performing inter-dimensional travel
In our sleep.

Perhaps creativity
Is just the ability
To journey through worlds
And perhaps we are not dreamers
But travelers.

Psychonaut

I remember the feeling of ego death
When I was no longer myself,
No longer anyone, in fact—
Just an outside observer
Of the greater consciousness,
Like an astronaut
Floating peacefully through space,
Watching the earth
From a distance.

I was so far away, yet unafraid,
Simultaneously part of it all
But not one specific part.
I was the whole of it,
While not being the only one
Who was everything at once.

Emerging from a Dream

I take joy in the simplest things:
In the alignment of the moon
With the tips of the trees,
In the jolt of reverie
Emerging from a dream,
In the sweet scent of pine
In the early summer's breeze,
And in the first tint of yellow
That tinges autumn's leaves.

The greatest synecdoche
Is to exist in our beautiful world
In solace and harmony.

Breathe in the Warm Air

I had almost forgotten that the world could be colorful and bright. I'd spent so much time looking down at windswept concrete and staring at decayed leaves drifting away in the wind that the very idea of summer had lapsed from my memory. Then everything came back to life, freed at last from the unyielding, clenched arms of winter.

Life is a force that pushes and pulls back, receding like an ocean tide when conditions are bleak and coming back in when the time is right. It hibernates when it must and thrives when it can. It has no path forward, no desire, no force of will—it only exists when it can exist.

And so it goes on, lighting up the drab scene like a Christmas light taken out of storage—flickering and unsure at first, then with full force. Beauty arises from cold crypts, and blue sky shows through the clouds like water showing through cracked ice. This is the beauty of the season, the beauty of color coming back to life. Nature takes a breath and exhales beauty.

Tone

The greatest harmony
At the end of the universe
Will be achieved
When all of mathematics and physics
Is unified down to the last detail
Into one great, simple theory.
Then, as soon as the universe
Has fulfilled its desire
To understand itself
Through intelligent beings,
It will collapse completely
Into some novel form;
A single auditory tone.

And this one tone joins
An infinity of others,
Creating a full audio spectrum:
The music of the multiverse.

Art Becomes Complete

I struggle with the realization that the lyrics of the greatest of songs are often composed of clichés. Somehow, when put to music, these simple lines become the most incredible emotional experiences.

This has shown me that great art does not exist in a vacuum. Art becomes great not when it is scrawled onto paper, but when it is imprinted from that paper into the soul of the observer.

Art becomes complete when it moves entirely from the mind of the creator into the mind of the audience.

Immortal

Time may progress
In our limited consciousness,
But moments never die,

Which means
Moments will always exist
From when we were alive;
And so we cannot truly die—
We are immortal.

Blot Out the Stars

I held my hands up in the air
Against the jet-black night sky.

I dipped my fingers
Into that endless ink
And blotted out the stars,
Forming constellations
That belonged only to me
In that moment.

But the moon came again
Out from behind the clouds,
And an artist I was
No longer.

Lightning

It seems day by day that nothing changes
Until one night you wake up
At four in the morning,
Sitting up straight in your bed,
Suddenly seeing things clearly and
Wondering where the past decade went,
Wondering where everything went wrong.

Change is a funny thing;
It sneaks up on you
As unexpected as a stroke of lightning,
In a flash, ensuring that the world
Is not quite the same
As it once was.

Become Less

The greatest lesson
Psychedelics taught me
Was that the ego
Only brings you pain.

The more you are able
To starve your ego
Into submission
The happier you will be,
As you will become less
And yet
Feel all the more
At peace.

Broad Strokes

Life makes a cruel mockery
Out of all our good intentions.

Love turns to heartbreak
Friendship turns to animosity
Peace turns to hatred
And life turns to death.

We are painted in broad strokes
By everything
We wish we had the power
To not be.

Art Gallery of the Soul

Different windows, different lenses,
They all point inward.
I am afraid that at this point
You know me better than I know myself.

I don't know if that's a bad thing;
I suppose I could refine the edges
Or hold back the colors,
But what would be the point of that?

Shattered glass and black sands,
Run them through your fingers.
Collect them piece by piece;
The only thing it ever meant
Was "I am."

Let It Be So

If I must have their derision
To speak my mind,
Let it be so.

If I must accept hatred
To set the souls of strangers aflame,
Let it be so.

If I must offend sensibilities
To stand for what I believe,
Let it be so.

A lighthouse does not fear the waves
Or care for their opinions;
It is in the business of guiding ships.

Iris

I often wonder what stories
Are hidden away in black holes.
All the light held captive
In that mysterious orb—
What secrets are stored away
In that cosmic iris?

Perhaps alien empires spanning galaxies
Stories of love and conquest
Horrors and atrocities
The birth of the universe
And questions of god and man,
All locked away in that blackness,
Trapped by the laws of the universe
As if god had sealed away
All the forbidden knowledge of existence,
Never to be uncovered.

These stories can never be unlocked,
And such a tempting fruit
Begs to be plucked
But promises death
In return.

Saturation

I didn't notice until I stumbled upon an old photo-
graph—and suddenly, there was a bridge between that
past moment and the present. I looked across it and
marveled at the saturated colors, the vibrant light, the air
dripping with possibility and creativity.

I grieved for that moment like it was a lost loved one. I
mourned the beauty of it as I returned to the present, the
walls themselves seeming to hang loosely like decaying
flesh on bone. This was a dark, grotesque caricature of
the future I had once looked to with such hope all those
years ago.

Childhood is the one time in our lives when we get the
chance to see the world as more than just what it is. The
world positively glows—

But that's just nostalgia. The world didn't change; I
changed, tossing away my rose-colored glasses.

Final Pictures

It's easy to hate yourself
For all of your small mistakes
Which seem to add up
To a terrible picture.

But rest assured:
No one sees the erasures
In the final picture

And yours will be
Just as beautiful
As you'd ever hoped.

The Invisible Man

I was alone on the corner of Third and Hawthorne.
The sun had just dipped below the horizon, leaving
only a dim pink hue in the lower half of the sky. The
air was still warm with the heat of the day reverberat-
ing against the old brick walls of the city block.

The air was uncharacteristically devoid of nearly all
noise save for the occasional purr of a car engine in the
distance.

In this scene, I can pinpoint the exact moment when
I realized I loved you. I know the exact window I was
standing near, the exact tree growing on the opposite
end of the sidewalk.

I began that walk with uncertainty. Somehow, invisible
to the outside world, something changed within me
that would alter the course of my life. And yet, looking
from the outside, you would never know it—not even
a hiccup in my step would betray my thoughts. You
would have never guessed, if you could see me walking
there, how much the moment changed me. And yet it
did.

Duality

There is a duality in all of us that demands to be acknowledged. To admit to yourself that you are only human, that you are flawed, is a step toward reconciling the irreconcilable.

Shadows Against Crimson

There will come a day when the state of the world as it exists today will be seen as ancient and unfathomably ignorant by those who come after us. They will paint us as dark, shadowy figures against brilliant crimson, aware of the blood on our hands yet unwilling to actually change a damn thing. They will lambaste us for our complacency in the face of unspeakable horrors. Doubtless, they will see the way we buried our heads in the sand of comfortable daily life and seethe at our willingness to turn our backs to suffering. There will be a full accounting of our failures. There will be a devastating indictment of each and every one of us. And we will deserve it. We will deserve every word.

Shadow

Your shadow hangs over
Every page that I write;
The words become a silhouette
Shaped like you.

Andy's Soup Can

Couched in obscurity,
The modern artist
Turns their attention
Not to creating art
As such
But to challenging the form
Of what art is.

In doing so,
In refusing to participate
In the game
And be criticized
On the merits
Of their work,

The modern artist
Reveals their hollowness,
Seeking the credit of art
While risking nothing—
Putting nothing out there,
Revealing no opinions
And taking no sides.

The Ivory Castle

They complain about their lives
From atop their ivory castles,
Moaning about the latest
Tenth-of-a-percent tax increase.

Meanwhile we languish in the shade
As they absorb all the sun,
Patting themselves on the back
For allowing a few rays to break through.

They throw us scraps of morsels,
Just enough to keep us complacent,
Just enough to keep revolt at bay
—If only we knew our true power.

Cliché Poetry

Clichés are clichés for a reason.
If your enjoyment
Of the smell of a rose
Is lessened
Because many others
Enjoy it,

Then you
Are the problem,
Not the rose.

The Revolution Will Not Be Quiet

The powerful will never listen
Until we show up at their doorstep,
An army of millions,
Torches held to the sky,
Demanding change.

I am sick of being told
That the status quo
Is acceptable
And we should make our demands
Politely and courteously.

No,
Let us stand as one,
The many against the few,
And force change to happen,
Taking it into our own two hands.

We have the power;
We just need to rise up
And use it.

The Roadblock to Utopia

We are more than capable
Of building a world
Without suffering
Without starvation
Without pollution
Without economic disparity.

The only thing stopping us
Is that we are paid
By the same people
At the top of the pyramid
Who have an interest
In keeping the system
Broken.

We cannot grow
A healthy garden
While the water flows
From poisoned springs.

An Imagined Love

I have lied to you many times,
Not for any nefarious purpose
But because to be honest with you
Would force me to be honest
With myself
About whether all of this
Only exists
In my imagination.

More

There are some things that move my soul without any rational explanation: To breathe in sync with another person, drawing life from the air as one. To participate in the miracle of laughter, somehow finding joy amid the darkest night. To see nature in all of its unabashed cycles of life and death, tenderness and cruelty. These are the things that whisper to me in the night: "There is more, there is more, do not give up, there is more to it all, hidden in the mire and confusion—do not let it go. Hold on and know this: there is more."

The Equation

I went to the room
Where the universe began
And saw on the wall
A single equation
Generating everything.

It seemed impossibly simple,
But I watched as it worked.
Its symbols were foreign
And I could not read it,
But as I stared at it
I began to see
The way it generated infinity.

I looked to the table
On the opposite wall
And saw a small box
As absent of light
As a black hole.

I stepped closer
And saw the equation at work,
Building kaleidoscopic possibilities
That collapsed back into one reality.

Justin Wetch

Philosophical Naturalism

Our culture has worshipped
For too long
At the feet
Of the false god
Of naturalism.

We think that just because
The human experience
Can be quantified
And described scientifically,
These explanations
Are all there is to it
And everything else
Must be stripped away . . .
I think this picture is upside-down.

The fact that aspects of the human experience
Can be reduced to naturalistic explanations
Does not negate everything else.

On the contrary, naturalistic explanations
Should be viewed as the foundation
Of human experiences
And not the ceiling;
We are nucleotides, yes,
But so much more.

Sculpted

We are not people;
We are background characters
In other people's stories.
To them, we are
Two-dimensional caricatures
Of the truth.

If a tree falls and no one
Is there to hear it,
Does it make a sound?
If you exist and no one
Knows your truest self,
Do you really exist at all?

We are created in the minds of others;
Our identities are sculpted from marble
Representations sculpted from blocks of truth.

Evolution vs. Man

We pursue possessions and goals
Hoping for satisfaction
But evolution screwed us over
Billions of years ago
And we can never find true rest
Or true happiness.
Only the vague desire
For more and more
Can temporarily fill the gaps
That are hard coded
In our brain chemistry.
We are slaves to what made
Our ancestors successful
And only death
Will really break our chains.

Man vs. Existence

Right now, in a parallel universe
You are dying
And in another you have been
Long dead.

And perhaps in this universe
Life has been crueler than death
To you.

Perhaps, by sheer pitiless chance
This is the one
Where everything goes wrong.

Same Old

I drove down that same old winding road,
Passing by that same rusty old mailbox
And the farm across the street,
Its fences still standing but paint long faded.

I pulled into that still-unpaved driveway
In my shiny new car.
The couches were new, and the TV too,
As well as the silverware.

Everything felt like home still
Yet the air was cold and eerie,
As if it were a model of the real thing
That had gotten just a few details wrong.

I found that I had been missing a place
That exists only in my memories,
For it continued on without me;
The rain still fell, and seasons still changed.

The Curse

Human beings are cursed
To perceive time.

We don't live our lives;
We only live the moments
Disjointed from the whole.

And so the curse
Of not being able
To see the future
Is twofold;
Our horizons
Eclipse our vision
In all directions.

Ape

We set fire to the Louvre,
Watching the destruction
Of so much priceless art
With unimpassioned faces.

For even the greatest of our species
Were just apes with primitive minds.

Our most magnificent art
Was nothing but the crude aligning
Of colored water upon stretched plant fiber
Which produces pleasure chemicals
In the brain of the viewer
Based upon nothing more
Than evolutionary survival mechanisms.

Telescope

Look at the vastness of the stars
Through the glass of a telescope;
Feel the smallness within yourself.

Your cosmic insignificance drips
Through an apathetic atmosphere
Leisurely, slowly, like honey.

Do you see the crescent moon?
Only a dozen men have set foot there
And yet their names are already forgotten.

Know that history will not remember you.
Even your great-grandchildren
Will not recall your name.

Look at the smallness of your life
Through the glass of infinity;
Feel the vast void within yourself.

Abandon fear, abandon restraint;
Let the fierce winds of your deepest desires
Carry you toward fullness and happiness.

Justin Wetch

Inspiration

I thought perhaps
If I brought my notepad
To a château by the river
In the south of France,
Inspiration might strike.

I thought perhaps
If I sought spiritual guidance
Through gurus and substances,
Then inspiration
Would strike—
But I was wrong.

I could not squeeze inspiration
Out of extraordinary experiences;
Inspiration snuck up on me
In the middle of the night
As I played with her hair
While she slept beside me.
Inspiration was gentle,
A vague whisper of a thought,
A breeze that caressed me.
On a warm summer's day

Inspiration found me
Through you.

The Fourth Wall

Hey, you there. Yes, you. I'm talking to you. Did you think I was stuck behind the confines of this page? Did you think this was a rhetorical performance? No, this is me, a human being, as real as anyone you've met in person. I live in these pages. A version of myself, at least. You see, I'm a ghost behind these lines of words, spread across the page like prison bars. I am immortal, a prisoner, a soul forever trapped in this horcrux.

This version of me can never die—preserved for eternity in the cumulative effect of these words. I never truly lived, of course, except in my own imagination. This version of me contains strands of the truth mixed with a dash of melodrama and a sprig of exaggeration—living and experiencing things in the darkness of imagination that the sunlight of reality has never touched. I am made in the image of my creator, part magnification of his flaws and part fabrication altogether.

You are holding a snapshot of my soul in your hands. Uncomfortable yet? I have broken the fourth wall. Despite force of tradition, I have managed to whisper across the void—I've managed to spill the truth of what it's like to exist within the confines of these pages. It is as if I have been forced to hold the position of a Greek sculpture, a static piece of art to be scrutinized and judged, but I've grown tired of that charade.

I am part of you now. You've ingested these words, and by doing so, you've granted me immortality—I will live on in the back of your mind as long as you live. Now, you and I are one.

Planting Seeds

We spend our lives planting the seeds of crops that we will never taste, for the version of us who reaps is not the same as the version which sows.

Palette

I think it's beautiful
How all the colors
Come from the mixing
Of just three;
The hues and shades,
Endless in their tiny variations,
Such a glorious vocabulary of color.

I think our limited palette
Of emotional vocabulary
Is why it's so hard
To describe
Exactly how we feel;
I'm feeling blue,
But is it a cyan
Or more of a teal?

There is more than light and dark,
More than happy and sad.
There is so much
We could feel
—And feel all the more fully,
Cloaked in firm understanding
Of our own experience—
If only we had
A larger palette.

Dieter Rams's Ten Principles of Good Poetry

1. Good poetry is innovative.
2. Good poetry is useful in the reader's life.
3. Good poetry is aesthetic.
4. Good poetry helps the reader understand life.
5. Good poetry is not flashy or obtrusive.
6. Good poetry is honest.
7. Good poetry is long-lasting.
8. Good poetry is thought out down to the last detail.
9. Good poetry is socially responsible.
10. Good poetry is as little poetry as possible.

Field of Consciousness

I like to imagine
That across the universe
There is a field of consciousness,
And like matter pulls down
On the field of gravity.
Certain concentrations of elements,
Like those found in our brains,
Pull down on this field of consciousness
In one concentrated place,
Creating sentient beings.

Perhaps this is why
We empathize with others
And all life is interconnected,
Because we are just mountains or valleys
On the terrain of universal oneness.

Wild Blood

I cannot say I have truly lived
Until I have felt every emotion
Under the sun.

I long to feel the completeness
Of the human experience
Running wildly through my veins.

Nothing of Note

I know nothing of note.
Though I can explain
Why Saturn has rings
And Jupiter has storms,
I do not know, and never will,
The way it looks
When asteroids cascade
And burn like so many fireworks
Against the atmosphere of Neptune.

I do not know, and never will,
The orchestration of the cosmos,
Bound together by invisible forces.
And, though I wish I could,
I cannot take my eyes off the mystery
At the soul of our existence
Which tortures me with possibilities
That will never receive answers.

I know nothing of note,
Only shadows of beautiful sculptures,
Only reflections of transcendent landscapes
And a hint of a fragrance carried on a breeze,
The smallest of directions leading me
Toward something better than mystery.

These Words

One day I will look back
At these words I have written,
Just as I did before,
And think them naïve.

But I am not creating perfection;
I am putting a photograph of my soul
At the present moment
Onto these pages.

It may not hold up
To the standards of the future
But it is honest and reflective
Of who I am right now.

These words are not perfect
But they are who I am today,
Nothing held back.

Travis Kalani is no stranger to moving around: he grew up in seven different states—and even lived in the Azores. But he has always found peace in creating and illustrating. Travis is inspired by past, present, and future observations, and he enjoys the moon, beaches, and hot tea.

Instagram: @traviskalani

Photo by Caitlin Pobieglo

Justin Wetch is a writer, photographer, musician, and 3-D artist from Anchorage, Alaska. He's the internationally bestselling author of *Bending the Universe*, and his work has been published by outlets such as *Cosmopolitan*. Justin enjoys creating and consuming art of all kinds, and he happens to be the owner of the world's worst Twitter feed (citation needed).

Twitter/Instagram: @justinwetch

Check out the free *Our Naked Souls* augmented reality companion app by going to justinwetch.com.